OpenStack

Creating Clouds

From Novice to Pro!

Table of Contents

# Introduction

Most companies and organizations now need to be able to control their resources via a cloud. The best cloud environment is the one which is easy for anyone to use and in which one gets what they want in terms of services and resources. OpenStack is a great solution for those who need to use a cloud environment in the easiest way. It offers you a number of resources which you can take advantage of so as to improve the operations of your organization. It is made up of a collection of a number of resources which are related to one another. Examples of the resources provided by the OpenStack include the compute service, the storage service, the image storage, and others. When one takes advantage of these resources and combines all of them, they are able to do much in their organization. It comes with an identity management service which helps to authenticate and authorize the users who try to access the system. It is only after a successful authentication that the users will be allowed to access the resources of OpenStack; otherwise, one will be denied access to these resources. This book guides you on how to use OpenStack. Enjoy reading!

# Chapter 1- Getting Started with OpenStack

OpenStack refers to a cloud operating system for controlling large pools of storage, compute, and networking resources via a datacenter, all of which are managed via a dashboard, through which the administrator exercises control and the users are empowered to provision the resources via a web interface.

This system is made up of several different systems which are separated. These services will always work together, and they include identity, networking, and compute, block storage, image, database services, orchestration, telemetry, and object storage. It is possible for you to install each of these services independently, and then configure them as stand-alone or in an entity manner.

Setting up the Environment

The majority of the environments have Image service, Identity, Dashboard Compute, and one or more networking services. However, the Object Storage Service is capable of operating independently. We will show you how to configure a controller and a compute node. Your dashboard will need at least the Compute, the Image Service, and Networking.

Each node must be configured from an account with administrative privileges. The commands must be executed by a "root" user or configure sudo tool.

The following are the minimum requirements for an environment capable of supporting the core and multiple CirrOS instances:

Controller Node: 1 processor, 5 GB storage, and 4 GB memory
Compute Node: 1 processor, 10 GB storage, and 2 GB memory

As you increase the number of OpenStack services and the virtual machines, the hardware requirements will also increase as a way of providing the best performance. Sometimes, the performance may degrade once you have added some additional resources. In this case, you should consider adding more hardware resources.

A minimal installation for a Linux distribution is the best for setting up OpenStack. Note that you have to install a 64-bit version for this in each of the available nodes. For a basic installation, some single basic installation on every node will work okay.

Security

There are a number of security methods which are supported in OpenStack. Examples of these include policy, password, and encryption.

In this case, we will be discussing password protection where it is possible. It is possible for you to generate some secure passwords manually, use a tool such as pwgen to generate them, or execute the command given below:

$ openssl rand -hex 10

Installing a Cloud Platform with OpenStack in CentOS 7/RHEL

For you to follow through with this, you should have a minimal installation of CentOS 7 or RHEL 7. You can then follow the steps given below:

Use your root account to login into the system and ensure that it is updated.

Run the command given below so as to show all the services which are running:

# ss –tulpn

You can then identify any services which are not needed and stop, disable, and then remove them. These include the NetworkManager, postfix and firewalld. You should only have the sshd daemon as the last one running on your computer. Just run the following sequence of commands:

# systemctl stop postfix firewalld NetworkManager
# systemctl disable postfix firewalld NetworkManager
# systemctl mask NetworkManager

# yum remove postfix NetworkManager NetworkManager-libnm

Run the commands given below so as to disable the Selinux on our machine. The "/etc/selinux/config" file should be edited, and the SELINUX line changed from "enforcing" to "disabled."

# setenforce 0
# getenforce
# vi /etc/selinux/config

The last command given above will open the file in the vi editor, so edit it as we said above. The line should be changed so as to appear as shown in the screenshot below:

```
#       permissive - SELinux prints warnings instead of enforcing.
#       disabled - No SELinux policy is loaded.
SELINUX=disabled
# SELINUXTYPE= can take one of three two values:
#       targeted - Targeted processes are protected,
```

You can then use the "hostnamectl" command as to the hostname for the Linux system. The FQDN variable should also be replaced:

# hostnamectl set-hostname cloud.centos.lan

You also need to be able to synchronize time with the NTP server. This calls for you to install the "ntpdate" command. Just run the command given below:

# yum install ntpdate

The rdo repository provides us with a PackStack package which can help us to deploy OpenStack.

For you to enable the rdo repository inside your RHEL system, just run the command given below:

# yum install **https://www.rdoproject.org/repos/rdo-release.rpm**

For CentOS 7 users, the Extras repository provides us with RPM, which will help us to activate the RPM repository. The Extras has been enabled, so the RPM can be installed for setting up the OpenStack repository:

# yum install -y centos-release-openstack-mitaka
# yum update –y

It is now a good time for you to install the PackStack package. It is a utility which will help us to perform deployment on a number of nodes for the different components of OpenStack through Puppet modules and SSH connections.

To install this package in your Linux system, just run the following command:
# yum install  openstack-packstack

You should then generate an answer file for your PackStack with default configurations which we will have to edit at a later time so as to have the type of configuration which is needed for standalone installation of the OpenStack. The file will be given a name which is similar to the current day timestamp after generation:

```
# packstack --gen-answer-file='date +"%d.%m.%y"'.conf
# ls
```

The anwer configuration file which has been generated should be opened and edited in a text editor. To open it, run the vi command plus the name of the as follows:

```
# vi 20.03.17.conf
```

The password fields should be replaced with the right thing. Replace the following line to appear as shown below:

```
CONFIG_NTP_SERVERS=0.ro.pool.ntp.org
```

You should ensure that you use a public NTP server which is near your geographical location. The following line should be edited as follows:

```
CONFIG_PROVISION_DEMO=n
```
Then the line is given below:

```
CONFIG_KEYSTONE_ADMIN_PW=password      for Admin user
```

You can then access the OpenStack Dashboard via HTTP with the SSL being enabled. This is shown below:

```
CONFIG_HORIZON_SSL=y
```

The MYSQL Server root password should be set as shown below:

```
CONFIG_MARIADB_PW=mypassword
```

You should be in a position to access the Nagios web panel. This calls for you to set the password for the nagiosadmin user as follows:

```
CONFIG_NAGIOS_PW=nagios
```

Once you are done with the editing, just close the file and ensure that you save everything. You can then open the configuration file for the SSH configuration file and ensure that you uncomment the section for "PermitRootLogin." You only have to remove the hastag located at the front of the line and you will have uncommented it. Open the file by running the following command:

# vi /etc/ssh/sshd_config

You can then uncomment the line so that it appears as follows:

Restart the service for changes to take effect:

# systemctl restart sshd

You can then use the PackStat Answer File so as to begin the installation of OpenStack as shown below:

# packstack --answer-file 20.03.17.conf

Once the installation has ran successfully and all the OpenStack components have been installed, the installer will show you a few lines together with links to the local dashboard, for Nagios and OpenStack as well as the other credentials which are needed for one to be able to login to the other panels.

The credentials will also be stored in the home directory and in the "keystonerc_admin" file.

Sometimes, the installation may fail and one gets an error regarding the httpd service. In such a case, just open the "/etc/httpd/conf.d/ssl.conf" file and then ensure that the following lines are commented. To comment, you only have to add a hash (#) at the beginning of the line as shown below:

#Listen 443 https

Restart the Apache daemon for changes to take effect. Just run the following command:

# systemctl restart httpd.service

In case you are still unable to browse the OpenStack web panel on port 443, restart your installation process from the start using the command which was issued for the initial deployment. Here is the command:

# packstack --answer-file /root/20.03.17.conf

For you to access the web panel for OpenStack from a remote host in the LAN, navigate to the machine IP address or the FQDN dashboard via the HTTPS protocol.

Since you are using a Self-Signed certificate which was issued by an untrusted Certificate Authority, you should see an error on your browser. You just have to accept this error, and then login by use of the admin user and the password which was set at CONFIG_KEYSTONE_ADMIN_PW parameter in your answer file.

**https://192.168.1.40/dashboard**

Also, if you had tried to install the Nagios components for the OpenStack, you just have to browse to the Nagios web panel by use of the URI given below, and use the credentials which you had set in the answer file:

**https://192.168.1.40/nagios**

You can now begin to setup your own internal environment for the cloud.

# Chapter 2- Identity Management

The OpenStack Identity Service provides us with a single point of integration for management of authentication and authorization. This is the first service which an OpenStack user has to interact with. It is after a successful authentication that the user finds it possible to gain access into the services of OpenStack.

Installation

Let us discuss the necessary steps for one to install and configure the identity service for OpenStack.

First, you should create a database and some administration token. The database can be created by doing the following:

Connect as the root to the database server:

$ mysql -u root −p

Create your keystone database:

mysql> CREATE DATABASE keystone;

Permit access to the keystone database:

mysql> GRANT ALL PRIVILEGES ON keystone.* TO 'keystone'@'localhost' \

  IDENTIFIED BY 'KEYSTONE_DBPASS';

mysql> GRANT ALL PRIVILEGES ON keystone.* TO 'keystone'@'%' \

  IDENTIFIED BY 'KEYSTONE_DBPASS';

The "KEYSTONE_DBPASS" should then be replaced with the right password. You can now the access client for the database.

Installing and Configuring Components

Install the packages by running the following command:

# apt install keystone

Edit the file "/etc/keystone/keystone.conf" so as to complete the actions given below:

Configure access to the database in the database section:

[database]
...
connection                                    =
mysql+pymysql://keystone:KEYSTONE_DBPASS@controller
/keystone

The "KEYSTONE_DBPASS" parameter should be replaced with the password which you created for the database. In the section for [token], configure the Fernet token as shown below:
[token]
...
provider = fernet

You can then go ahead and populate the database for the identity service:

# su -s /bin/sh -c "keystone-manage db_sync" keystone

Now, initialize key repositories for Fernet as shown below:

# keystone-manage fernet_setup --keystone-user keystone --keystone-group keystone

# keystone-manage credential_setup --keystone-user keystone --keystone-group keystone

Run the following command so as to bootstrap the identity service:

```
# keystone-manage bootstrap --bootstrap-password ADMIN_PASS \

  --bootstrap-admin-url http://controller:35357/v3/ \
  --bootstrap-internal-url http://controller:35357/v3/ \
  --bootstrap-public-url http://controller:5000/v3/ \
  --bootstrap-region-id RegionOne
```

The "ADMIN_PASS" parameter should be replaced with the right password for the administrator user.

Configuring Apache HTTP Server

You should edit the "/etc/apache2/apache2.conf" configuration file as well as the ServerName option so that it can reference the controller node:

ServerName controller

Restart your Apache service, and then get rid of the default SQLITE database:

```
# service apache2 restart
# rm -f /var/lib/keystone/keystone.db
```

Now, configure details for the administrative account:

```
$ export OS_USERNAME=admin
$ export OS_PASSWORD=ADMIN_PASS
$ export OS_PROJECT_NAME=admin
$ export OS_USER_DOMAIN_NAME=Default
$ export OS_PROJECT_DOMAIN_NAME=Default
$ export OS_AUTH_URL=http://controller:35357/v3
$ export OS_IDENTITY_API_VERSION=3
```

The 'ADMIN_PASS" parameter should be replaced with the password which was used in the previous "keystone-manage bootstrap" command.

# Chapter 3- Network Configuration

We can now configure the network for OpenStack so that we may be able to access the OpenStack instances. After this configuration, external networks will also be in a position to access the OpenStack instances.

Modify the Configuration Files for the Network Interface

Before you can begin to create the networks for the OpenStack on the dashboard, you should begin by creating an OVS bridge and then modify the physical network interface so as to bind as a port to the OVS Bridge.

Login to the terminal of the server, navigate to the directory with the network interface scripts, and then make use of the physical interface as the excerpt for setting up the OVS bridge interface simply by running the commands given below:

```
# cd /etc/sysconfig/network-scripts/
# ls
# cp ifcfg-eno16777736 ifcfg-br-ex
```

You can then use a text editor so as to edit a bridge interface. Open it by running the command given below:

```
# vi ifcfg-br-ex
```

Below is an excerpt for the interface br-ex:

```
TYPE="Ethernet"
BOOTPROTO="none"
DEFROUTE="yes"
IPV4_FAILURE_FATAL="no"
IPV6INIT="no"
IPV6_AUTOCONF="no"
IPV6_DEFROUTE="no"
IPV6_FAILURE_FATAL="no"
NAME="br-ex"
```

```
UUID="1d239840-7e15-43d5-a7d8-d1af2740f6ef"
DEVICE="br-ex"
ONBOOT="yes"
IPADDR="192.168.1.41"
PREFIX="24"
GATEWAY="192.168.1.1"
DNS1="127.0.0.1"
DNS2="192.168.1.1"
DNS3="8.8.8.8"
IPV6_PEERDNS="no"
IPV6_PEERROUTES="no"
IPV6_PRIVACY="no"
```

The same should be done to the eno16777736 physical interface, while ensuring that it is as follows:

```
TYPE="Ethernet"
BOOTPROTO="none"
DEFROUTE="yes"
IPV4_FAILURE_FATAL="no"
IPV6INIT="no"
IPV6_AUTOCONF="no"
IPV6_DEFROUTE="no"
IPV6_FAILURE_FATAL="no"
NAME="eno16777736"
DEVICE="eno16777736"
ONBOOT="yes"
TYPE="OVSPort"
DEVICETYPE="ovs"
OVS_BRIDGE="br-ex"
```

As you edit the interface cards, ensure that you have replaced the name for the interface, the IPS, and the DNS server names.

Once the changes have been done, just restart the network daemon by use of the ip command so as to ensure that your changes take effect:

```
# systemctl restart network.service
```

# ip a

Creating a New Project

At this point, we should use the OpenStack dashboard so as to configure the cloud environment. Login to the OpenStack dashboard or web panel using the admin credentials.

You should create a new project by navigating through "Identity -> Projects -> Create Project."

Projects

You should then create a new user by navigating through "Identity -> Users -> Create Use" and fill in all the details which are required for the new user. The Role for this new user should be assigned as the "_member_ ."

Configuring the Network

It is now time for us to configure the network for OpenStack. Once you are through with the creation of the user, log out of the dashboard as the admin, and then log in as the new user so as to be able to create your two new networks.

Navigate through "Project -> Networks -> Create Network," and then configure your internal network as shown below:

Network Name: internal
Admin State: UP
Create Subnet: checked
Subnet Name: internal-tecmint
Network Address: 192.168.254.0/24
IP Version: IPv4
Gateway IP: 192.168.254.1
DHCP: Enable

It will also be good for you to replace the Network Name, the Subnet Name, and the IP addresses with the custom settings.

You can then follow our previous steps so as to create an external network. The IP address space for your external network must be in a similar range as the IP address range for the uplink bridge interface so as to work in the right way without the extra routes.

This means that if br-ex interface has 192.168.1.1 as the default gateway for the 192.168.1.0/24 network, this same network and the gateway IPs must be configured for the external network too.

This is shown below:

Network Name: external
Admin State: UP
Create Subnet: checked
Subnet Name: external-tecmint
Network Address: 192.168.1.0/24
IP Version: IPv4
Gateway IP: 192.168.1.1
DHCP: Enable

Again, ensure that you have replaced the Network Name, the Subnet Name, and the IP address based on your custom configurations.

In our next step, we should log into the OpenStack dashboard as the admin and then mark the external network as the External so as to be able to establish communication with the bridge interface.

Login as the admin, and then navigate through Admin -> System-> Networks, click external network, and then check the box External Network. Click on "Save Changes" so as to save the changes which you have just made.

Once done, log out the admin user, and then login as an ordinary user so as to proceed with the next steps.

We should now be looking for a way to facilitate movement of packets from one network to another. This can only be achieved by creation of a router. Navigate through "Project -> Network -> Routers," and then click on the button for "Create Router." You should then add the settings given below to your router:

Router Name: a descriptive name for the router
Admin State: UP
External Network: external

After the router has been successfully created, you will see it in the dashboard. Click on the name of the router, open the tab for "Interfaces," and then click on the button for "Add Interface.".You will see a new prompt popup.

Choose the "internal subnet," leave the field for the IP Address empty,  and then click on the "Submit" button so that the changes can be applied. You will see your interface change its state to active after a few seconds.

For you to verify the network settings for OpenStack, navigate to the Project -> Network -> Network Topology and you will see a network map presented to you.

At this point, you will have your OpenStack network functioning, and capable of receiving traffic from virtual machines.

# Chapter 4- Creating, Deploying and Launching Virtual Machines

In this guide, we will guide you on how to create images, launch the instance of the image or the virtual machine in OpenStack, and then gain control over the instance via SSH.

Allocation of a Floating IP to the OpenStack

Before the deployment of an OpenStack image, all units must be in the right place, and we should begin by allocation of a floating IP.

The work of a Floating IP is to allow for external access or an Internet to an OpenStack virtual machine. For you to create the Floating IPs for the project, begin by logging into the system, navigate through "Project -> Compute -> Access & Security -> Floating IPs," and then click on the option for "Allocate IP" to your project.

Select "External" pool, then click the button for "Allocate IP," and you will see the IP address in your dashboard. It is always good for you to allocate a Floating IP to every instance that you run.

Creation of an OpenSTack Image

The OpenStack images refer to virtual machines which have been created by third parties. It is possible for you to create customized images on the machine by installation of a Linux OS in the virtual machine by use of a virtualization tool such as VMware, VirtualBox, KVM, or Hyper-V.

After installation of the OS, the file should be converted to raw and uploaded to the OpenStack cloud infrastructure. Ensure that you install only the official images which are provided by the Linux distributions.

In this chapter, we will be deploying the attest image which is based on a CirrOS cloud image (lightweight). You can use this image on the **http://download.cirros-cloud.net/0.3.4/** link or just download it and then upload to the OpenStack cloud.

For you to create an image, open the web panel for OpenStack, then navigates through "Project -> Compute -> Images," and click on the button for "Create Image." A prompt will pop up, so use the settings given below:

Name: nicohsam-test
Description: Cirros test image
Image Source: Image Location  #Use Image File if you have downloaded the file locally on your hard disk

Image Location: **http://download.cirros-cloud.net/0.3.4/cirros-0.3.4-i386-disk.img**

Format: QCOWW2 – QEMU Emulator
Architecture: leave blank
Minimum Disk: leave blank
Minimum RAM: leave blank
Image Location: checked
Public: unchecked
Protected: unchecked

Once done, click on the button for "Create Image."

Launching Image into the OpenStack

Now that the image has been created, it is okay for you to move ahead. It is possible for you to run the virtual machine based on the image which you created earlier in the cloud environment.

Navigate through "Project -> Instances," then click on the "Launch Instance" button, and you will see a new window popup. In the first screen, type in the name for your instance, but leave the value for the "Availability Zone" set to nova. Use a single instance count, and then click the "Next" button so as to proceed.

Choose a descriptive "Instance Name" for the instance, since this is the name which will be used for forming the hostname for your virtual machine.

Next, choose the image as "Boot Source," and then add the "Cirros" test image which you had created earlier simply by clicking on the + button. Once done, click on "Next" so as to proceed.

Allocate the resources for the virtual machine by adding a flavor which best suits your needs, and then click the "Next" button so as to proceed.

You can then add one of OpenStack networks which are available to the instance by clicking on the + button, and then click on the button for "Launch Instance" so as to start the virtual machine. After the launching of the instance, click the right arrow found on the "Create Snapshot" menu button, and then select "Associate Floating IP."

Choose one of the floating IP which you had created earlier, and then click on the "Associate" button so as to ensure that the instance can be reached from the internal LAN.

You can then use the Ping command so as to test for the network connectivity for the active virtual machine against the floating IP address from the remote computer in the LAN.

In case the instance has no issue and the Ping command runs successfully, you can login remotely via SSH into the instance.

label: Key name

description: Name of key-pair to be used for compute instance

```
    default: my_key
  private_network:
    type: string
    label: Private network name or ID
    description: Network to attach instance to.
    default: private-net

resources:
  my_instance:
    type: OS::Nova::Server
    properties:
      image: { get_param: image }
      flavor: { get_param: flavor }
      key_name: { get_param: key }
      networks:
        - network: { get_param: private_network }

outputs:
  instance_ip:
    description: IP address of the instance
    value: { get_attr: [my_instance, first_address] }
```

In the template given above, we have added two other top-level sections which include the following:

parameters- we use this to define the list of inputs which will be provided by the user.
outputs- this defines the attributes of the stack which will be exported once a deployment has been done.

When we use the parameters section, it becomes easy for us to make the template generic. Each of the used parameters has to be given a name plus a type, a description which is optional, and a value. The function "get_param" is used when we need to insert some parameter values into the resource properties. The function "get_attr" is used in the section for outputs when we need to extract the resource attributes which we desire for the ones which have been included in the stack.

It will be good for you to try this new template, so just save it as "heat_1b.yaml," and then start it as we have shown you below. Note that in our template, I used the parameter values which match the installation of my OpenStack. If you have not used the same values, then you have to edit the template values so as to match your installation, otherwise, you will get an error. However, rather than editing the values of the parameters used in the template, it is possible for you to specify the right values in the command line via the command given below:

(venv) $ heat stack-create second_stack -f heat_1b.yaml -P "key=key_name;image=Trusty"

In the above command, the value of the key parameter has been set to "key_name," while the value for the image parameter has been set to "Trusty." This means that these are the values which will be used for the instantiation of the stack. For the rest of the parameters which have not been specified in the −P option, then the default ones will have to be used as defined in the template. This means that you should get the ones which are incorrect in the template and specify their correct values on the command line via the −P option. In our case, this will apply to the flavor and the private network values as you have not specified them in the command line. Note that in the case of parameters with no default values, we have to define their correct values in the "stack-create" command, which means that we have a good way of defining the defaults whenever it is possible.

After a successful creation of the stack, just run the "stack-show" command so as to show all the attributes which you request in the output section. The command should be as shown below:

(venv) $ heat stack-show second_stack

# Chapter 6- Single Instance Deployments in OpenStack

In this chapter, we will guide you on how to use Heat to perform single deployments for applications.

Application Deployment on First Boot

The cloud-init package forms the de facto standard for the initialization of the cloud instances. In most cloud images, this comes pre-installed. The cloud-in it will run once an instance has been booted for the first time, and it will check from the Nova metadata service API for any actions which are expected to be done.

The easiest way for you to interact with this is by giving it a script which will be run during boot time. The execution of this script will be done as a root user, which means it will have full access to an instance to install, and then apply any configuration changes where necessary. Consider the template given below, which is simply an extension of the "heat_1b.yaml" template we had earlier:

heat_template_version: 2013-05-23

description: Simple template for deploying a single compute instance

parameters:
  image:
    type: string
    label: Image name or ID
    description: Image for use for the compute instance
    default: cirros-0.3.3-x86_64
  flavor:
    type: string
    label: Flavor
    description: Type of instance (flavor) to be used
    default: m1.small
  key:

```
  type: string
  label: Key name

  description: Name of key-pair to use for the compute
instance

  default: my_key
 private_network:
  type: string
  label: Private network name or ID
  description: Network to attach instance to.
  default: private-net

resources:
 my_instance:
  type: OS::Nova::Server
  properties:
   image: { get_param: image }
   flavor: { get_param: flavor }
   key_name: { get_param: key }
   networks:
    - network: { get_param: private_network }
   user_data: |
    #!/bin/sh
    echo "Hello, World!"
   user_data_format: RAW

outputs:
 instance_name:
  description: Name of the instance
  value: { get_attr: [my_instance, name] }
 instance_ip:
  description: IP address of the instance
  value: { get_attr: [my_instance, first_address] }
```

In our template given above, we have made a few changes
including the following:

The property "user_data" on the "my_instance" resource will have a small initialization script which will print a greeting message.
The property "user_data_format: RAW" tells Heat script to give a "user_data" script to the instance with no additional contents.
The output "instance_name" will export the name which was assigned to the instance.

To try the above template, you just have to run the command given below. Remember to save it with the name "heat_2a.yal":

```
(venv) $ heat stack-create stack_with_init_script -f heat_2a.yaml
```

However, it may happen that some of the values for the parameters are not right for your environment. In this case, you should use the –P option so as to specify the right values for these parameters. Suppose you had named your private network as "private," and you need to use an image named "Trusty," you only have to specify them as shown in the command given below:

```
(venv) $ heat stack-create stack_with_init_script -f heat_2a.yaml -P "private_network=private;image=Trusty"
```

You should now verify whether your user data script has been executed or not. You just have to access the output of the command from the console log of the instance by use of the nova command line client. For us to obtain the console log, we should first obtain the name which was assigned to the instance by Heat, and then we have a look at the stack outputs:

```
(venv) $ heat stack-show stack_with_init_script
```

Once you have learned the instance name, you can obtain the console log by running the command given below:

(venv)    $    nova    console-log    stack_with_init_script-my_instance-t5elvfeqdz63 | less

Scroll down the log and identify the "Hello, World!" message which was printed by the initialization script. Once you are done with experimenting with the stack, you can delete it by running the command given below:

(venv) $ heat stack-delete stack_with_init_script

An Actual Deployment

We need to demonstrate an actual deployment by use of a template which has been written in Python for the deployment of a web application. This will be achieved by the use of Flash microframework. This is an application which works with sending email notifications, database, implementing an API, and it provides us with a modern web interface. Below is our deployment template:

heat_template_version: 2013-05-23

description: A template for deploying a Flasky single instance server with SQLite database.

parameters:
  image:
    type: string
    label: Image name or ID

    description: Image for server use. Use an Ubuntu-based image.

    default: trusty-server-cloudimg-amd64
  flavor:
    type: string
    label: Flavor

```
  description: Type of flavor (instance) to be used on compute
instance.

  default: m1.small
 key:
  type: string
  label: Key name

  description: Name of the key-pair to be installed on compute
instance.

  default: my_key
 private_network:
  type: string
  label: Private network name or ID
  description: Private network to attach the server to.
  default: private-net
 gmail_username:
  type: string
  label: Gmail account username

  description: Username of Gmail account to be used for
notifications.

 gmail_password:
  type: string
  label: Gmail account password

  description: Password of Gmail account to be used for
notifications.

  hidden: true

resources:
 flask_secret_key:
  type: OS::Heat::RandomString
  properties:
   length: 32
    sequence: lettersdigits
```

```
flasky_instance:
  type: OS::Nova::Server
  properties:
    image: { get_param: image }
    flavor: { get_param: flavor }
    key_name: { get_param: key }
    networks:
     - network: { get_param: private_network }
    user_data_format: RAW
    user_data:
      str_replace:
        params:
          __gmail_username__: { get_param: gmail_username }

          __gmail_password__: { get_param: gmail_password }

          __flask_secret_key__: { get_attr: [flask_secret_key,
value] }
        template: |
          #!/bin/bash -ex

          # install dependencies
          apt-get update

          apt-get -y install build-essential python python-dev
python-virtualenv nginx supervisor git

          # create some flasky user for running the server process

          adduser --disabled-password --gecos "" flasky

          # clone flasky from github
          cd /home/flasky
          git clone https://github.com/miguelgrinberg/flasky.git
          cd flasky

          # Write configuration file
          cat >.env <<EOF
```

```
FLASK_CONFIG=heroku
SECRET_KEY=__flask_secret_key__
```

DATABASE_URL=sqlite:////home/flasky/flasky/appdb.sqlite
```
MAIL_USERNAME=__gmail_username__
MAIL_PASSWORD=__gmail_password__
FLASKY_ADMIN=__gmail_username__@gmail.com
SSL_DISABLE=1
EOF

# create virtualenv then install dependencies
virtualenv venv
venv/bin/pip install -r requirements/prod.txt
venv/bin/pip install gunicorn==18.0

# create database
venv/bin/python manage.py deploy

# make a flasky user to be owner of the application
chown -R flasky:flasky ./
```

# configure the supervisor for running private gunicorn web server,

# to autostart this on boot and after it crashes

# stdout and stderr logs from server will go to the /var/log/flasky

```
mkdir /var/log/flasky
cat >/etc/supervisor/conf.d/flasky.conf <<EOF
[program:flasky]

command=/home/flasky/flasky/venv/bin/gunicorn -b 127.0.0.1:8000 -w 4 --chdir /home/flasky/flasky --log-file - manage:app

user=flasky
autostart=true
```

```
autorestart=true
stderr_logfile=/var/log/flasky/stderr.log
stdout_logfile=/var/log/flasky/stdout.log
EOF
supervisorctl reread
supervisorctl update

# configure nginx to be front-end web server with some
reverse proxy

# rule to gunicorn server
cat >/etc/nginx/sites-available/flasky <<EOF
server {
    listen 80;
    server_name _;
    access_log /var/log/nginx/flasky.access.log;
    error_log /var/log/nginx/flasky.error.log;
    location / {
        proxy_pass http://127.0.0.1:8000;
        proxy_redirect off;
        proxy_set_header Host \$host;
        proxy_set_header X-Real-IP \$remote_addr;

        proxy_set_header                    X-Forwarded-For
\$proxy_add_x_forwarded_for;

    }
    location /static {
        alias /home/flasky/flasky/static;
    }
    location /favicon.ico {
        alias /home/flasky/flasky/favicon.ico;
    }
}
EOF
rm -f /etc/nginx/sites-enabled/default

ln -s /etc/nginx/sites-available/flasky /etc/nginx/sites-
enabled/
```

```
        service nginx restart
```

```
outputs:
  instance_name:
    description: Name of instance
    value: { get_attr: [flasky_instance, name] }
  instance_ip:
    description: IP address of deployed instance
    value: { get_attr: [flasky_instance, first_address] }
```

Save the template as "heat_2b.yaml." After that, use the following command so as to launch it:

```
(venv) $ heat stack-create flasky -f heat_2b.yaml -P
"gmail_username=<gmail-user>;gmail_password=<gmail-
pw>"
```

As usual, if you need to use different values for the parameters, just specify them using the "-P" option. The two parameters which have been specified above were not supplied with default values in the template, so we have to specify their values.
In the template, you should have noticed that we have two parameters which are asking you to provide the credentials for your Gmail account. The Flasky application usually sends emails to the users so as to notify them of some of the events. This is why we are using a third party solution such as Gmail. However, in a production environment, do not use the Gmail service. The credentials for this will be kept in a configuration file inside the instance, but they will not be available in the logs. This is because we have used the "hidden: true" property.

Although our application is now running fully, we have not connected it to the outside world.

Network Implementation

Although most of the work has been done in the template, very little has been done on the networking part. The template will only serve to connect the instance to the private network which you specify. The port 80 has not been opened to the external clients, and we have done nothing so as to assign some floating IP which can be accessed by the external clients.

Creating a Security Group

Heat provides us with a resource type whose work is to help us create a security group for an instance. Below is a change which should be made to our template:

```
resources:
  ...
  web_server_security_group:
   type: OS::Neutron::SecurityGroup
   properties:
    name: web_server_security_group
    rules:
     - protocol: tcp
       port_range_min: 80
       port_range_max: 80
     - protocol: tcp
       port_range_min: 443
       port_range_max: 443
     - protocol: icmp
     - protocol: tcp
       port_range_min: 22
       port_range_max: 22

  flasky_instance:
   type: OS::Nova::Server
   properties:
     ...
    security_groups:
     - { get_resource: web_server_security_group }
```

The use of the "OS::Neutron::SecurityGroup:" helps us specify the ports which should be opened and the property "security_groups" will link to this. In our case, we have opened ports 80 and 443.

Creation of a Private Network

At this, telling a private network to attach an instance is not very convenient. The reason is because we don't have a proper way of telling the Heat that the network has been properly configured, and it has been routed to the external network. In our example here, we will not specify a private network in existence, but the template will ask for an external network which can be asked as the source of the floating IP address. When given this information, the template will create its own private network, and a router for connecting it to the external world.

Below we have the changes. The parameter "private_network" should be replaced with a new one known as "public_network," and we have added a few resources for creation of the net, subnet, and the router as shown below:

```
parameters:
  ...
  public_network:
    type: string
    label: Public network name or the ID

    description: A public network with a floating IP addresses.

    default: public-net
  ...

resources:
  ...

  private_network:
    type: OS::Neutron::Net
```

```
private_subnet:
  type: OS::Neutron::Subnet
  properties:
    network_id: { get_resource: private_network }
    cidr: 10.10.10.0/24
    dns_nameservers:
    - 8.8.8.8

router:
  type: OS::Neutron::Router
  properties:
    external_gateway_info:
      network: { get_param: public_network }

router-interface:
  type: OS::Neutron::RouterInterface
  properties:
    router_id: { get_resource: router }
    subnet: { get_resource: private_subnet }
```

Note that we began by creating a new net, subnet, and the router resources. Our network will be routed to an external network, so a DNS address is needed for name resolution. In the case of the router, the parameter "public_network" has been specified to be the gateway. Our fourth resource is "router-interface," and we will be using it for associating our private network with the router.

Assigning a Floating IP Address

We should now allocate a floating IP address to our server. The following change can help us accomplish this:

```
resources:
  ...
  flasky_port:
    type: OS::Neutron::Port
    properties:
```

```yaml
      network: { get_resource: private_network }
      security_groups:
        - { get_resource: web_server_security_group }

  flasky_instance:
    type: OS::Nova::Server
    properties:
      ...
      networks:
        - port: { get_resource: flasky_port }

  floating_ip:
    type: OS::Neutron::FloatingIP
    properties:
      floating_network: { get_param: public_network }

  floating_ip_assoc:
    type: OS::Neutron::FloatingIPAssociation
    properties:
      floatingip_id: { get_resource: floating_ip }
      port_id: { get_resource: flasky_port }

outputs:
  ...
  instance_ip:
    description: IP address of deployed instance
    value: { get_attr: [floating_ip, floating_ip_address] }
```

Note that the template has been changed so that we can attach the server to a port. The resource "OS::Neutron::FloatingIP" has helped us to assign the floating IP address. The resource "OS::Neutron::FloatingIPAssociation" has then been used to associate the floating IP address to the port.

You can now combine all the codes into a single template, and then run the following command so as to launch it:

```
(venv) $ heat stack-create flasky -f heat_2c.yaml -P
"gmail_username=<your-gmail-
user>;gmail_password=<gmail-pw>"
```

You can also use the exact name for your external network if
you didn't use the default one we have used in this case.

Signaling

After all that, you must have realized that Heat is not aware of
all the operations involved in the deployment. The reason
behind this is that the stack will be switched to a state of
"STACK_COMPLETE" once the instance has been launched,
and it will not wait for the installation script which is under
execution to complete. Heat has no way of telling what the
script is doing, but it is capable of passing this script to the
instance and assuming that the completion will happen soon.
However, the fact that we don't know the exact time for
completion of deployment causes a problem.

However, there are a number of ways that an instance can
send back signals to Heat API so as to inform it about the
progress of installation process. To solve this, add the
following to your template:

```
resources:
  ...
  wait_condition:
   type: OS::Heat::WaitCondition
   properties:
    handle: { get_resource: wait_handle }
    count: 1
    timeout: 600

  wait_handle:
   type: OS::Heat::WaitConditionHandle

  flasky_instance:
   type: OS::Nova::Server
```

```
  properties:
    ...
    user_data:
     str_replace:
      params:
        ...
        wc_notify: { get_attr: ['wait_handle', 'curl_cli'] }
       template: |
        #!/bin/bash -ex
        ...
        wc_notify --data-binary '{"status": "SUCCESS"}'
```

The resource "OS::Heat::WaitCondition" will instantiate some special resource which can be signaled via a handle from the instance.

# Conclusion

We have come to the end of this book. OpenStack is an operating system for the cloud controlling a large pool of resources such as compute, storage, and networking resources. Note that all of these services are done through a datacenter, and the administrator is provided with a dashboard through which he can exercise the necessary control. OpenStack is an open source tool, which makes it an ideal tool for many users in cloud computing. The development of this tool was done to act as Infrastructure as a Service (IaaS). OpenStack is made up of related components which are good for the control of diverse and multi-vendor hardware tools for storage, processing, and networking via the datacenter. To manage the OpenStack, one can use the command line tool, the web interface, or a RESTful API.

www.ingramcontent.com/pod-product-compliance
Lightning Source LLC
Chambersburg PA
CBHW070903070326
40690CB00009B/1971